Argentina

Suzanne Paul Dell'Oro

Carolrhoda Books, Inc. / Minneapolis

Photo Acknowledgments

Photographs, maps, and artworks are used courtesy of: John Erste, pp. 1, 2–3, 9, 12–13, 19, 23, 24–25, 29, 32–33, 39, 41, 42–43; Laura Westlund, p. 4, 7; © TRIP/D. Saunders, pp. 4–5; © SuperStock, pp. 6 (left), 10; © M. Joly/D. Donne Bryant Stock, p. 6 (center); © Fritz Pölking/Visuals Unlimited, p. 6 (right); © Robert Fried, pp. 7, 12, 13 (both), 16 (left), 18, 22, 24, 28, 29 (left), 31 (both), 35 (left); © Roberto Bunge/D. Donne Bryant Stock, pp. 8, 35 (top right); © C. Goldin/D. Donne Bryant Stock, pp. 9 (left), 16 (center and right), 21 (top), 23 (top), 29 (right), 32, 35 (bottom), 39, 42, 44, 45; © Jean S. Buldain, p. 9 (right); Archive Photos, p. 11 (top); UPI/Corbis-Bettmann, p. 11 (bottom); © Schulte/D. Donne Bryant Stock, pp. 14, 40 (bottom); © Victor Englebert, p. 15 (left); © TRIP/J. Drew, p. 15 (right); Hugo Dell'Oro, pp. 17, 20, 21 (bottom), 25, 43; © TRIP/M. Barlow, pp. 19, 41; © Charles W. McRae/ Visuals Unlimited, pp. 23 (bottom), 33 (bottom); © William Banaszewski/Visuals Unlimited, p. 26 (left); Reuters/Wilson Malo/Archive Photos, p. 26 (right); © Mary & Lloyd McCarthy/Root Resources, pp. 27 (top), 30 (left); Press Association/Archive Photos, p. 27 (bottom); © M. Long/Visuals Unlimited, p. 29 (center); © R. Sanguinetti/ D. Donne Bryant Stock, p. 30 (right); © Michel Gotin, p. 33 (top); © Max & Bea Hunn/SuperStock, p. 34; © Michael Moody/D. Donne Bryant Stock, p. 36; painting by Florencio Molina Campos, p. 37 (top); © Mrs. Jane H. Kriete/Root Resources, p. 37 (bottom); © Allan A. Philiba, p. 38; © TRIP/A. Ghazzal, p. 40 (top). Cover photo of La Boca neighborhood, © Michael Moody/D. Donne Bryant Stock.

Carolrhoda Books, Inc.
c/o The Lerner Publishing Group
241 First Avenue North
Minneapolis, Minnesota 55401 U.S.A.

Website address: www.lernerbooks.com

Words in **bold type** are explained in a glossary that begins on page 44.

Library of Congress Cataloging-in-Publication Data

Dell'Oro, Suzanne Paul.
    Argentina / by Suzanne Paul Dell'Oro
       p. cm. — (Globe-trotters club)
    Includes index.
    Summary: An overview of Argentina, emphasizing its cultural aspects.
    ISBN 1–57505–114–1 (lib. bdg. : alk. paper)
    1. Argentina—Juvenile literature. [1. Argentina.] I. Title. II. Series:
Globe-trotters club (Series)
F2808.2.D45 1998
982—dc21   97–41568

Manufactured in the United States of America
1 2 3 4 5 6 – JR – 03 02 01 00 99 98

Contents

BOLIVIA

PARAGUAY

Iguazú Falls

BRAZIL

A N D E S

Tucumán

A R G E N T I N A

Paraná River

Córdoba

Rosario

URUGUAY

Mendoza

Aconcagua

Buenos Aires

Río de la Plata

C H I L E

PAMPAS

Mar del Plata

ATLANTIC OCEAN

Legend

~ mountains
— plains
··· plateau
/// Lake District

Miles
0 100 200 300 400

0 200 400 600
Kilometers

Bariloche

P A T A G O N I A

VALDÉS PENINSULA

PACIFIC OCEAN

N

Moreno Glacier

TIERRA DEL FUEGO

CAPE HORN

¡Bienvenidos a la Argentina!*

*That's "Welcome to Argentina" in Spanish, the official language of Argentina.

Look at a map of the world. Can you find Florida in the southern United States? Use your finger to draw a straight line from Florida all the way down to the

The Moreno Glacier in Patagonia creeps slowly across the land.

tip of **South America.** There's Argentina! It's four times as big as Texas, and it's the second largest country, after Brazil, in South America.

Argentina has many neighbors. It shares the tip of South America with skinny Chile. To the east and south lies Argentina's biggest neighbor, the Atlantic Ocean. Bolivia, Paraguay, Brazil, and Uruguay surround Argentina's northern side. About 435 miles south of Argentina is Antarctica—the coldest place on earth. You can find almost any type of landform you can imagine in Argentina—from beaches to **glaciers.**

Because Argentina is located south of the **equator,** its seasons are opposite those in North America. Summer starts in November, and winter comes in June!

5

Mount Aconcagua (far left) **is part of the towering Andes. Andean peoples** (center) **have accepted the challenge of mountain living. A tropical rain forest hides among the Andes** (above).

The Backbone of **Argentina**

The Andes, the world's longest mountain range, run through Argentina. They hold Mount Aconcagua— the highest peak outside Asia! The Andes start far north of Argentina in Panama and reach all the way to the southern tip of South America. The range runs north and south like a backbone along Argentina's western side. The country's tailbone is in the water.

Iguazú Falls

Much of the land on the eastern slopes of the Andes is cactus-covered **desert.** Mountains trap rain clouds coming from the west, making the eastern Andean slopes dry and windy. But nestled among the mountains on the eastern side in Tucumán—like a hidden treasure—is a **tropical rain forest.** The heavy rainfall helps tropical plants grow easily, which gives Tucumán its nickname, the Garden of the Nation.

Life is tough in the mountains, but the locals make the best of it. Because traveling is difficult, most mountain people haven't been to Argentina's cities. Perhaps that's why the Andean lifestyle hasn't changed in many years.

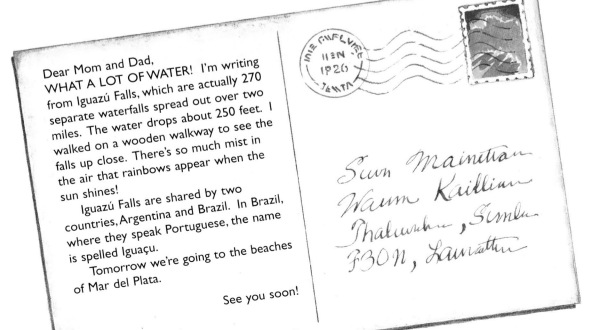

Dear Mom and Dad,
WHAT A LOT OF WATER! I'm writing from Iguazú Falls, which are actually 270 separate waterfalls spread out over two miles. The water drops about 250 feet. I walked on a wooden walkway to see the falls up close. There's so much mist in the air that rainbows appear when the sun shines!
   Iguazú Falls are shared by two countries, Argentina and Brazil. In Brazil, where they speak Portuguese, the name is spelled Iguaçu.
   Tomorrow we're going to the beaches of Mar del Plata.

See you soon!

Home on **the Range**

Most of eastern Argentina has flat **plains** that seem to go on forever. The central plains region is called the **pampas.** Many crops, like wheat, corn, and soybeans, grow in the rich soil. Huge herds of sheep and cattle munch on the lush grass that covers most of the pampas. More than half of Argentina's 35 million people live in big cities in the pampas region.

Argentina's southern plains—known as Patagonia—take up most of the lower third of the country. Only about 1 million people live there—and it's no wonder why. The cold, dry conditions and poor soil make Patagonia a harsh place to live. Few crops grow, but ranchers raise sheep on the grassy **plateaus** (high, flat land) to sell the wool and meat. Parts of Patagonia are beautiful. For example, the Lake District has green pine forests and crystal clear lakes fed by rivers of melting mountain snow.

A rocky plateau rises out of the dry Patagonian landscape.

Look on the map on page 4. Do you notice a small group of islands to the south of Patagonia? That region is known as Tierra del Fuego, which means Land of Fire. How did it get its name? When European explorers sailed nearby long ago, they saw fires shining along the shore. The Indians who lived there built those fires for warmth and for cooking. And that's how Tierra del Fuego got its name.

The crystal clear waters of the Lake District attract tourists from around the globe.

Sheep and cattle graze on the grasses of the pampas, where some of the world's fastest racehorses are also raised.

Q: Why are the pampas like the letter N?

A: They're both in the middle of "Argentina"!

Buenos **Aires**

Avenida 9 de Julio (July 9 Avenue)—the widest avenue in the world—cuts through downtown Buenos Aires.

Do you remember reading that most Argentines live in the cities of the pampas? Well, that's where you'll find Argentina's largest city, Buenos Aires. If you look at the map on page 4, you'll see Buenos Aires, where the Río de la Plata meets the Atlantic Ocean. In Spanish, Río de la Plata means "river of silver." But unlike its name suggests, the river is not made of silver.

Buenos Aires is a port city, where ships from all over the world can dock to load and unload goods. The Buenos Aires **metropolitan area** has more than 11 million people! People who live there are nicknamed *porteños* (port people).

Buenos Aires has old-fashioned buildings with balconies at every window and fancy carved-stone decorations. Beside them are modern skyscrapers and high-rise buildings. They might hold businesses, homes, movie theaters, department stores, or government offices.

10

Picture the White House, where the president of the United States lives and works. Imagine it pink! Argentina's president works in the Casa Rosada (Pink House).

Madres de la Plaza

A square in Buenos Aires is called the Plaza de Mayo (May Plaza). Once a week, a group of women march in the plaza to remember a sad time in Argentina's history. They are known as the Madres de la Plaza (Mothers of the Plaza). During the 1970s and early 1980s, the government of Argentina was closely linked to the army. Thousands of people who disagreed with the government disappeared, without any explanation, after being arrested. Most people believe that the *desaparecidos* (missing), as they are known, died in jail. But the Mothers of the Plaza want the government to explain what happened to their loved ones.

Getting Around **in Argentina**

Argentines are on the go. Trucks transport beef, wheat, corn, and other grains from the pampas to markets throughout the country or to the port in Buenos Aires. From there, ships take goods across the ocean for sale. Trucks also haul fruit, wine, and wool across the countryside.

But people have a different way of getting around. In crowded cities like Buenos Aires, there's not room for everyone to have a car. Streets are filled with traffic jams, so many people prefer to ride Subte, the underground train system, or subway. Buses and taxicabs carry people through the city, and walkers crowd the sidewalks.

In small towns, people travel on horseback, by bicycle, or by car. In

Cars clog Avenida 9 de Julio.

Buses and subways whisk city people to wherever they want to go.

rural areas, dirt roads become rivers of mud when it rains! The only vehicles that can get through the muck are horse-drawn carts or very old cars with skinny tires. More modern inventions just spin their wheels!

13

The First **Argentines**

Thousands of years ago, the first Argentines came to the country. They are known as *indios*, or Indians. There were several different groups of Indians, each with its own language and customs. Although very few Indians are alive these days, Argentina still holds clues to their past. Museums display clay pots and stone weapons that the Indians made. Many rivers, mountains, and lakes in southern Argentina have Indian names—names like Nahuel

Modern-day Indians live mostly in the mountains. Others live in small communities in Patagonia and in northern Argentina.

Huapí (a lake) and Yumu Yumu (a river).

When Spanish settlers came to Argentina hundreds of years ago, they forced many Indians to work on farms. Some Indians were killed by the Spanish, while others died of sicknesses that the Spanish unknowingly brought with them. Over time Spanish and Indian people married and formed famlies. Their children and their children's children are called *mestizos*.

Hands Down

Several caves in Argentina have evidence of early Indian cultures. Paintings on cave walls include dancing or hunting scenes and footprint and handprint tracings. Can you guess what paintings decorate the walls in La Cueva de las Manos, meaning "Cave of Hands"?

Make your own cave paintings:
1) Lay a tan piece of paper, such as a grocery bag, on a flat surface.
2) Place your hand, fingers spread, on the paper.
3) Use a cut-up sponge to dab brown, red, or white poster paint around the shape of your hand.
4) Lay your hand down again at a different angle and repeat the painting in another color.

Which hand is easier to paint? Most of the hand tracings in La Cueva de las Manos were adult-sized left hands—probably made by right-handed artists.

A newsstand (left) displays papers with some of the languages spoken in Argentina.

A Land of **Many Languages**

Although Argentina's official language is Spanish, you can hear dozens of other languages spoken in cities and towns across the country. Each of Argentina's Indian populations communicates in one of 17 different languages! You might also hear people using English, Polish, German, Korean, or Italian, just to name a few. But almost everybody can speak Spanish.

Argentina is a land of newcomers. Hundreds of years ago, ships

Silver Lining

More than 400 years ago, the Spanish came to South America in search of riches. They had hoped to find silver in southern South America, and named the land Argentina from the Latin word for silver, *argentum*. (Several European languages, including Spanish, are based on the old language of Latin.) Although they didn't find much silver, the Spanish found something even better—rich grasslands of the pampas.

brought Spanish settlers to Argentina. Since then more and more people from different countries have arrived. Each group has added something special to Argentine culture. **Immigrants** brought with them words, food, and customs. Many Argentines enjoy Italian food like ravioli and lasagna.

One group that never quite mixed in with Argentine society is *los gitanos*, the Gypsies. Although no one is quite sure where the Gypsies came from, it is believed they came to Argentina from Eastern Europe. They mostly keep to themselves, traveling from one town to the next, camping just outside the city limits. You might see women in long, colorful dresses and scarves shopping for food. Gypsies speak their own language and follow their own traditions.

Gypsy homes are portable, so they can be moved from place to place.

Speaking **Spanish**

As you know, Argentines speak Spanish. In Spanish some letters have different sounds than you might think. For example, the letter *j* sounds like *h*, as in the name José (hoh-SAY). The *h* in Spanish is silent.

While the English alphabet only has 26 letters, the Spanish alphabet has 29. Here are three new letters for you to learn. The letter *ñ* (EN-yay) makes a sound like the *nyeh* in onion. Try to say the word *mañana* (mah-NYAH-nah). That means "tomorrow." The letter *rr* (ER-rray) sounds like a stick being dragged across a picket fence. It's a hard sound for many English-speaking people to say. In Argentine Spanish, the letter *ll* (EHL-yay) makes a sound like the *zsh* in treasure. Try to say the word *ella* (AY-zshah), meaning "she."

Students on a school field trip take a break to talk with their friends.

How Names Work

When a woman gets married, she keeps her last name. But she also adds *de* (of), plus her husband's last name. For example, Rosa García marries Guillermo Moreno. Rosa's new name would be Rosa García de Moreno. Guillermo's name stays the same. Their children's last name will be Moreno.

Argentines enjoy making up colorful sayings. If someone is tagging along after another person, he or she is "following like a dog follows a horse cart." A teacher's pet is called a "sock sucker." When storekeepers ask too much money for something, they're "taking your head off" with their prices.

The Plaza de Mayo in Buenos Aires is a popular spot to stop and chat.

How Words Work

Here are some words you can say to an Argentine:

hello	*hola*	(OH-lah)
pleased to meet you	*mucho gusto*	(MOO-choh GOO-stoh)
good-bye	*chau*	(CHOW)
yes	*sí*	(SEE)
no	*no*	(NOH)
see you later	*hasta luego*	(AH-stah loo-WAY-goh)

Two young Argentine cousins enjoy an afternoon snack break with their grandparents. Grandfather sips mate, a traditional Argentine drink.

Family **Traditions**

Family life in Argentina is very important. An Argentine child not only lives with his or her parents, brothers, and sisters, but also with grandparents, uncles, or aunts. That way, there's always someone to keep an eye on the kids. Who lives in your home?

In addition to these family members, many Argentine children have godparents. Each child's *madrina* (godmother) and *padrino* (godfather) help raise him or her, giving advice, love, and gifts.

Family togetherness helps make sure that traditions continue. For example, when an Argentine girl turns 15 years old, the family spends a lot of time preparing for a special birthday party called a *cumpleaños de quince* (there's that crazy letter ñ again). The party plans begin months in advance, arranging for special food and a fancy new dress. This birthday party is a way for the family to recognize that the girl is reaching an age when she will soon be a grown woman. ¡*Feliz Cumpleaños*! means "Happy Birthday" in Spanish.

20

All in the Family

Here are the Spanish words for family members. Practice using these terms on your own family. See if they can understand you!

grandfather	*abuelo*	(ah-BWAY-loh)
grandmother	*abuela*	(ah-BWAY-lah)
father	*padre*	(PAH-dray)
mother	*madre*	(MAH-dray)
uncle	*tío*	(TEE-oh)
aunt	*tía*	(TEE-ah)
son	*hijo*	(EE-hoh)
daughter	*hija*	(EE-hah)
brother	*hermano*	(ehr-MAH-noh)
sister	*hermana*	(ehr-MAH-nah)

Friends and family members help an Argentine girl celebrate her cumpleaños de quince (fifteenth birthday). At the party, guests eat cake and dance to music.

21

City families live in high-rise apartment buildings. People too poor to afford an apartment may live in *villas miserias*, or slums, on the edge of the city.

Argentine for
a Day

What would it be like to live in Argentina for a day? Well, it would depend a lot on where you live. City kids live with their parents in high-rise apartments. After school they may take karate or tennis lessons, meet their friends at playgrounds for a game of soccer, or watch television. Kids who live on a ranch spend lots of time outdoors. They learn to ride a horse at an early age to help tend to the animals. In small towns, kids live with their family in a house and play in the town's large open park, called a plaza.

Besides school and play, Argentine children help their parents with chores. If a child's parents own a store, he or she would probably spend some time at the check-out counter or watch younger brothers and sisters while the parents work. Country kids help to run the family farm by feeding animals or picking vegetables.

Since Argentines don't sit down for dinner until 10:00 P.M., kids enjoy *merienda* (afternoon snack) at 6:00 P.M. They share a plate of cake or crackers and wash down the snack with a glass of milk or tea.

Nap Time

From 12:00 P.M. until 3:00 P.M. —the hottest part of a summer day—towns close down for a siesta (nap). Shops and businesses reopen in the afternoon and stay open until 7:00 at night. Dinner is usually served after 10:00! The siesta has become a tradition, and people take this daily break all year... not just in summer. Even in the city, with its air-conditioned buildings, many people take this time to eat lunch and relax during a busy day.

A local park offers children a place to run and play (top). Daily activities include doing chores (left), too. Don't you wish you had a horse to help take out the trash?

Summer **School?**

While you're on summer vacation, Argentine kids are still in school, or *en la escuela*. Remember reading that seasons there are opposite from the ones in the United States? The school year is, too. School starts in March and ends in December. Argentine kids have summer vacation between December and March, while you're in class.

Teachers and students wear smocks, called *guardapolvos*, to keep their clothes clean during school. Guardapolvos means "keep off the dust." Kids from the same school wear matching guardapolvos, so you can tell what school they go to.

Students put on guardapolvos when they get to school. Field trips during the school day are a fun way to learn.

Argentine students study math, science, history, art, and reading. After spending the morning at school, kids go home for lunch and to take a siesta.

The school day is only four or five hours long. Since lots of kids attend one school, half of the kids goes to school in the morning, and the other half goes in the afternoon. That way they can be at home during the siesta and can help out with the family chores.

Line Up!

This song is sung to preschoolers as they learn to line up. They put their hands on the hips of the child in front of them and march in a long line.

*The centipede is a
    strange bug.
It looks like many bugs
    stuck together.
I look at it and it reminds
    me of a train.
I count its feet and they
    add up to 100.*

A *Sporting* **Chance**

Soccer is a favorite sport of many Argentines.

One of soccer's most famous players, Diego Maradona (above), got his start in Argentina.

Argentine *fútbol* players don't wear padding or helmets. Why not? Because fútbol is the Spanish word for soccer—the number-one sport in Argentina! Argentines are wild about soccer. They ask, "Are you a fan of Boca or River?" They mean, for which soccer team from Buenos Aires do you root—the Boca Juniors or River?

Paddle anyone? That's what Argentines call tennis, another popular sport in Argentina. Gabriela Sabatini, an Argentine tennis star, dazzled tennis fans in the 1990s. Many towns have at least one tennis court so that promising superstars can practice their backhand.

Argentina's mountains attract sports fans, like adventurous climbers and skiers, from around the

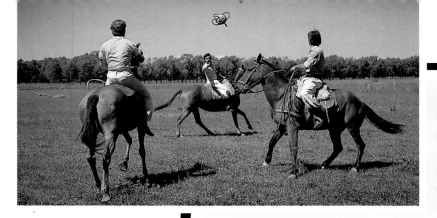

Playing with Horses

Throughout history Argentines have worked and traveled on horseback. It's not surprising that they use horses to play sports, too! In the English game of polo, players on horses use mallets to knock a ball toward a goal. Argentine cowboys invented *pato*. Originally players on horseback tried to move a live pato (Spanish for "duck") in a bag toward a goal by reaching down for the bag with their hands. These days players use a leather ball with many handles on it.

world. Climbers try scaling Mount Aconcagua. Skiers shoosh down the slopes at Las Leñas ski area near Mendoza.

Former tennis superstar Gabriela Sabatini takes a swing.

Relaxing in **Argentina**

How do kids in Argentina have fun? Pretty much the same way you might. They ride bikes, build go-carts, and watch their favorite television shows. In the summer, kids can swim all day at the local public pool. Or if they live near the ocean, they can take a trip to the beach.

Many kids enjoy getting together with kids in their neighborhood for a game of fútbol. (The word for soccer, remember?) They play at a nearby field. Other kids might prefer roller-skating at the local gymnasium. Some skaters belong to teams that practice after school and compete with other teams.

In the country, children find different ways to have fun. Most of them learned to ride a horse when they were young. They may know how to throw a lasso, which is a rope with a loop in the end. If they get good at it, they might compete in a rodeo, called a *jineteada*. "¡Arre! ¡Arre!"

Look familiar? Hanging out with friends seems to be a good way to pass the time anywhere in the world.

A young Argentine practices to compete in a rodeo (far left). **Roller-skating** (center) **or playing soccer** (below) **are two great ways to spend a sunny afternoon.**

Sea Serpent Game

In the game "La Víbora De La Mar" (the Sea Serpent), children form a long line and hold the waist of the person in front of them. They are the serpent. Two other children join hands above their heads to make a bridge. As they sing, the serpent passes under the bridge. The children who are the bridge suddenly drop their hands during the last line of the song to catch one of the children in the serpent. Can you think of a game like this? Maybe "London Bridge Is Falling Down"?

29

On *Vacation*

Where does your family like to go on vacation? Argentines enjoy traveling in their own country. There's a lot to see! Vacationers might make a day-trip to a shopping mall, to a neighboring town, or to visit family members. Others may plan a fishing excursion. In northern rivers, fishers can try their luck at catching a *dorado*—South America's strongest river fish weighing up to 60 pounds!

Whether vacationing in Mar del Plata (top left) **or hitting the ski slopes** (above) **in the Lake District, Argentines have many wonderful places to visit.**

Or they can try deep-sea fishing off the coast of Mar del Plata.

Vacationers who want to feel like traveling to another country but don't have the time can visit Bariloche, located in the Lake District of Patagonia. Bariloche is built to

If you're going to Bariloche, save room for its famous chocolate.

look like a town in Germany. The Argentine version, like the German one, is famous for its chocolate and its ski slopes. Other favorite tourist sites include the wine-making city of Mendoza, and Córdoba, a large city in the pampas.

Bariloche's Clock Tower

In the middle of Bariloche's main plaza stands the town hall, which has a clock tower. Every day at noon, the clock chimes, and out pop four wooden statues that rotate as the clock strikes. The statues are of an Indian, an early settler, a Spanish soldier, and a priest. They represent figures important in Argentina's history.

The Gaucho **Spirit**

Gauchos chose their clothing for its comfort and style. The outfit includes baggy pants called *bombachas*, a broad-brimmed hat, and a *rastra* (belt covered with coins).

"¡Arre! ¡Arre!" If you've ever seen a movie about the Wild West, then you know of the rugged lifestyle of the North American cowboy. Argentines have their own cowboy, called a gaucho.

In the old days, gauchos worked on the open range of the pampas, roping cattle and living off the land. They ate raw beef from a freshly killed cow and dried beef called *charqui* (jerky). Famous for their excellent horse-riding skills, they spent their days riding across the countryside with their cattle. Each gaucho carried a weapon, called a *boleadora*, made of stones attached to a leather cord. To trap a runaway animal, a mounted gaucho would

The Mate Tradition

Gauchos drank a tea called mate. Mate is prepared in a small, hollow gourd (hard-skinned squash) by pouring boiling water over yerba mate (crushed tea leaves). After the tea cools, mate is sipped through a *bombilla*—a metal straw with a bulb at the end that strains out the leaves.

Mate doesn't have to be prepared in a gourd. It can be made in anything from a tin mug to a silver cup. Mate is the national drink of Argentina, but younger kids probably prefer a tall glass of soda pop.

throw the boleadora so it would wrap around the legs of a running steer and trip it.

Argentines have many folktales and songs about gauchos. They admire the gauchos' ability to do a lonely, difficult job in the wilderness and to lead an honest life. Although true gauchos don't exist anymore, modern-day gauchos can show off their cattle-roping techniques at rodeos.

In the 1800s, ranch owners fenced in the land. Gauchos were no longer needed to keep the herds together. People living in the country still carry on some ways of traditional gaucho lifestyle.

Keeping the **Beat**

Music and dance tell the history of Argentine people. One gaucho folk dance, *el escondido*, tells a story of a gaucho who must hide from his enemies. Musicians play the accordion-like *bandoneón*, and dancers wearing traditional gaucho-style clothing clap their hands, stomp their feet, and clack a boleadora to keep time. Other traditional songs and dances include the *malambo* and the *zapatéo*.

A sad type of dance and music called the tango originated years ago in the slums, or poor neighborhoods, of Argentine cities. The

Dancers wearing traditional gaucho clothing perform a folk dance.

Modern Music

There is plenty of modern music in Spanish. The radio plays songs by stars like Luís Miguel, Julio Iglesias, and the Gypsy Kings. Some singers mix the old and the new. Mercedes Sosa, Atahualpa Yupanqui, and Leon Gieco are popular singers who base many of their songs on traditional music. *Confiterías,* or discos, open at 1:00 A.M. and play music until dawn. Young people also enjoy dancing and listening to bands from the United States and Europe—even if they don't understand the words.

Two musicians play the sad music of the tango (left). **Mastering the zampoñas** (above) **takes a lot of practice. Two dancers strike a typical tango pose** (below).

tango tells about life in the slums and of lost love. People dance complicated, dramatic steps to it. Like gaucho music, many tangos are played on the bandoneón. Besides the bandoneón, traditional music is played on *zampoñas* (panpipes), the *chorango* (short guitar-like instrument), and the *quena* (flute).

Argentine **Art**

Where can you find art in Argentina? Well, you could go to the National Museum of Fine Arts. Or you could just walk through the streets of La Boca, a Buenos Aires neighborhood.

La Boca is an unusual neighborhood with brightly colored homes, where artists have lived for many years. In an alleyway known as El Caminito (Little Passageway), artists have painted huge pictures, called

La Boca neighborhood was once a slum until artist Benito Quinquela Martín turned things around. He built a school there on the condition that it also house a museum for local artists.

Animated Art

Florencio Molina Campos (1891–1959) was an artist whom Argentines love because of his paintings of country and gaucho life. He painted in a cartoon-like style that got him a job with Walt Disney. He's also known for his beautiful landscape paintings of the pampas.

Artists have created scenes of Argentine life on the walls in San Telmo. Don't try this at home!

murals, on outdoor walls. You can buy artwork in an open-air market in El Caminito and in another neighborhood called San Telmo.

Traditional crafts in Argentina include wool scarves, leather bags, wooden plates, gaucho belts, and double-layered sheepskin slippers. These goods are sold in markets and in tourist shops.

Dinner time! Meat roasted slowly over an open-pit barbecue sends mouthwatering smells into the air.

Tasty **Treats**

Argentines eat more beef than people in any other country in the world, and it's eaten at nearly every meal! Argentines prepare beef in lots of different ways, but one of the most common ways is to barbecue it over an open fire. Meat prepared this way is called *asado*. It might be served with a slice of crusty bread, cooked potatoes, and a salad of lettuce or tomatoes and onion. Argentines also barbecue pork, lamb, fish, chicken, and turkey.

Empanadas, which are pastries filled with hamburger, raisins, olives, and spices, make good snacks. Argentines satisfy their sweet tooth with *dulce de leche* or with slices of cheese served with jellied fruit. Dulce de leche is made from milk and sugar. It cooks on the stove until it thickens and has a caramel color and taste. It is the most popular of sweets, and Argentines use it for everything from frosting cakes and cookies to making dulce de leche ice cream.

Although cities have supermarkets, most Argentines shop at specialty stores, like butcher shops and bakeries for fresh meat and fresh bread. Believe it or not, Argentina has stores, called *galletiterías*, that sell only crackers and cookies.

A waiter serves a plate of *ñoquis* and other typical Argentine foods.

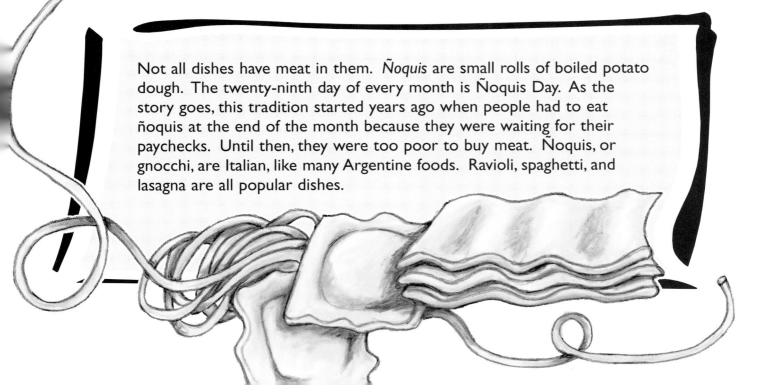

Not all dishes have meat in them. *Ñoquis* are small rolls of boiled potato dough. The twenty-ninth day of every month is Ñoquis Day. As the story goes, this tradition started years ago when people had to eat ñoquis at the end of the month because they were waiting for their paychecks. Until then, they were too poor to buy meat. Ñoquis, or gnocchi, are Italian, like many Argentine foods. Ravioli, spaghetti, and lasagna are all popular dishes.

Church and
Beliefs

In Argentina, most people belong to the Roman Catholic Church. Although many Argentines do not go to church regularly, religion is part of everyday life. Sometimes people show their faith in small ways. They say, "if God wishes," when they hope something will happen. Many people carry prayer cards with a picture of a saint, whom they believe will protect them against bad luck.

Many holidays in Argentina are based on Christian religious festivals. On December 25, Argentines celebrate Christmas. Families share *pan dulce*, a sweet bread with raisins and nuts, served only at Christmas. Like Santa Claus, Papá Noel visits

Catholic churches (top) are found in even the most deserted places. During a religious parade (left), townspeople carry a float with a statue of their patron saint.

children on Christmas Day. But the gifts children really look forward to come 12 days later on Three Kings' Day. In the Christian belief, three wise kings gave gifts to the baby Jesus on this day. Children leave their shoes outside so that the kings will leave them gifts, too.

Argentine Roman Catholics chat after attending a Sunday service.

Water by the Road

As one Argentine folktale goes, a young mother and her baby from the Correa family were lost in the desert without water. The woman died, but her baby was able to nurse milk from its mother until rescuers arrived.

To many Argentines, La Difunta Correa (meaning "the dead Correa") is a story of a miracle and about giving up something for another person. Along Argentina's highways there are bottles of water set carefully by the roadside. Travelers and local people put them there in memory of La Difunta Correa and pray for her help in business, love, and health.

Special Days

Argentines don't wait for religious occasions to enjoy holidays. They find lots of reasons to party! People from different regions hold festivals to celebrate what feature makes their land famous.

Vendimia, for example, takes place in a town in the Andes, where one-fifth of the world's wine grapes grow. In early March, festival-goers celebrate the grape harvest. During the three-day event, a priest blesses the grape vines. Later there is a parade, and local vineyards serve free wine.

Grapes for making wine thrive in sunny Mendoza, where Vendimia—the wine celebration—is held each year.

In July, during skiing season, the town of Bariloche holds a Snow Festival. A downhill skiing competition takes place during the day, and music and a torchlight parade on skis happen at night. It's a frosty party for those who love the snow.

In the first week of December—Argentina's summer—residents of Mar del Plata celebrate the National Sea Festival. Argentines enjoy sporting events, a ceremony to bless the sea, bonfires, and the crowning of the Queen of the Sea.

Carlos Gardel

Dancing in the Streets

The first two weeks of January are reserved for the Tango Festival. A town outside of Buenos Aires hosts an international crowd of visitors that celebrate the music and dance made famous in Argentina. Carlos Gardel, the most celebrated Argentine tango musician, is a folk hero to Argentines and tango lovers. Although he is no longer alive, his talent lives on. His portrait decorates many walls and billboards throughout the country.

Colorful umbrellas at Mar del Plata give hundreds of tourists protection from the sun.

Glossary

desert: A dry, sandy region that receives low amounts of rainfall.

equator: The line that circles a globe's middle section halfway between the North Pole and the South Pole.

glacier: A sheet of ice formed by thousands of years of snowfall, and which grows larger when new layers of ice and snow never melt away. As the bottom layers of ice melt and refreeze, the glacier moves slowly across the land.

immigrant: A person who moves from their home country to another country.

metropolitan area: A central city and the towns (suburbs) that have grown up around it.

pampa: A large area of flat, grass-covered land located in South America, east of the Andes.

plain: A broad, flat area of land, usually covered by grass, that has few trees or other outstanding natural features.

plateau: A region of level land that is above most of the surrounding territory.

South America: The large body of land, located mainly below the equator, and includes the countries of Argentina, Brazil, Peru, and Chile.

tropical rain forest: A dense, green forest that receives large amounts of rain every year. These forests lie near the equator.

This house is located in Ushuaia in Patagonia. Ushuaia is the southernmost town in the world!

The Legend of Luján

In 1630 a wagon carrying a statue of Mary, the mother of Jesus, became stuck in muddy banks of the Luján River. The oxen pulling the wagon wouldn't budge. As the owner jostled the cart free from the mud, the statue fell from the wagon. The owner reloaded the statue, but the oxen again refused to move. The owner believed this was Mary's way of saying that she wanted the statue to stay put. He built a chapel around the statue that was later replaced by a larger church. Some people even walk the 40 miles from Buenos Aires to show their devotion the Virgin of Luján.

Pronunciation Guide

Aconcagua	ah-cohn-CAH-gwah
Argentina	ahr-hehn-TEE-nah
bandoneón	bahn-doh-nay-OHN
Bariloche	bah-ree-LOH-chay
bienvenidos	byehn-veh-NEE-dohs
boleadora	boh-lay-ah-DOH-rah
bombilla	bohm-BEE-zhah
Buenos Aires	BWEH-nohs EYE-rays
Córdoba	COHR-doh-bah
cumpleaños de quince	koom-play-AH-nyohs day KEEN-say
desaparecidos	day-sah-pah-ray-SEE-dohs
dulce de leche	DOOL-say day LAY-chay
galletiterías	gah-zsheh-tee-teh-REE-ahs
gitanos	hee-TAH-nohs
guardapolvos	gwahr-dah-POHL-vohs
Iguazú	ee-gwah-SOO
jineteada	hihn-ay-tay-AH-dah
La Difunta Correa	lah dee-FUHN-tah coh-RRAY-ah
La Víbora de la Mar	lah VEE-boh-rah day lah MAHR
Madres de la Plaza	MAH-drays day lah PLAH-sah
mate	MAH-tay
merienda	meh-ree-EHN-dah
Nahuel Huapí	NAH-well wha-PEE
ñoquis	NYOH-kees
porteños	pohr-TAY-nyohs
quena	KAY-nah
Río de la Plata	REE-oh day lah PLAH-tah
Tierra del Fuego	tee-YEHRR-ah dehl FWAY-goh
Tucumán	too-koo-MAHN
zampoñas	zahm-POH-nyahs
zapatéo	zah-pah-TAY-oh

Further Reading

Argentina in Pictures. Minneapolis: Lerner Publications Company, 1994.

Belleville, Cheryl Walsh. *Rodeo.* Minneapolis: Carolrhoda Books, 1985.

Brusca, Maria Cristina. *My Mama's Little Ranch on the Pampas.* New York: Henry Holt and Company, Inc., 1994.

Brusca, Maria Cristina. *On the Pampas.* New York: Henry Holt and Company, Inc., 1991.

Hintz, Martin. *Argentina.* Chicago: Children's Press, 1985.

Mendel, Peter. *Material World: A Global Family Portrait.* San Francisco: Sierra Club Books, 1994.

Parnell, Helga. *Cooking the South American Way.* Minneapolis: Lerner Publications Company, 1991.

Peterson, Marge and Rob. *Argentina: A Wild West Heritage.* Minneapolis: Dillon Press, Inc., 1990.

Metric Conversion Chart

WHEN YOU KNOW:	MULTIPLY BY:	TO FIND:
teaspoon	5.0	milliliters
Tablespoon	15.0	milliliters
cup	0.24	liters
inches	2.54	centimeters
feet	0.3048	meters
miles	1.609	kilometers
square miles	2.59	square kilometers
degrees Fahrenheit	5/9 (after subtracting 32)	degrees Celsius

Index